Yakety Sax

WORDS AND MUSIC BY JAMES RICH AND BOOTS RANDOLPH

Sony/ATV Music Publishing

EXCLUSIVELY DISTRIBUTED BY

HAL•LEONARD®
CORPORATION
7777 W. BLUEMOUND RD. P.O. BOX 13819 MILWAUKEE, WI 53213

YAKETY SAX

Words and Music by JAMES RICH
and BOOTS RANDOLPH

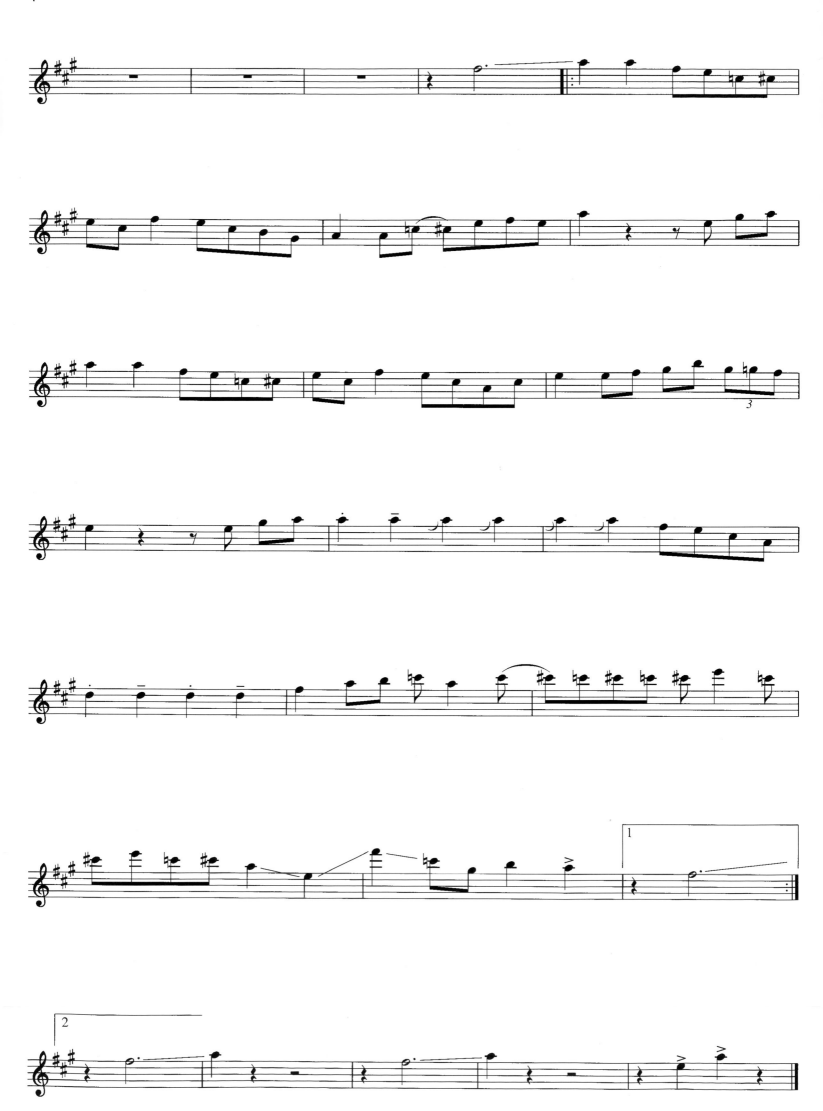

B♭ TENOR SAX
with Piano Accompaniment

Yakety Sax

WORDS AND MUSIC BY JAMES RICH AND BOOTS RANDOLPH

Sony/ATV Music Publishing

EXCLUSIVELY DISTRIBUTED BY

HAL•LEONARD®
CORPORATION

7777 W. BLUEMOUND RD. P.O. BOX 13819 MILWAUKEE, WI 53213

YAKETY SAX

Words and Music by JAMES RICH
and BOOTS RANDOLPH

Moderately fast

*Tenor Sax part sounds one octave lower than written.